born palestinian,
born black

suheir hammad

 UpSet Press, Inc.
P.O. Box 200340
Brooklyn, NY 11220
www.upsetpress.org

UpSet Press is an independent, not-for-profit, tax-exempt (501c3) small press based in Brooklyn, New York. The mission of the press is to support and showcase innovative and progressive work by emerging writers (first/second books), as well as to restore to print rare and out-of-print works (again with a special focus on first/second books). Founded in 2000 by a group of Brooklyn-based poets, the press intends to publish one to two books annually. In addition to its publishing endeavors, the press conducts regular poetry workshops and readings around New York City. For more information regarding the press; submissions, queries, internships, book purchases, etc., please visit upsetpress.org.

First printing, 2010
ISBN 978-0-9760142-2-5
Library of Congress Control Number: 2010933475
Printed in the USA
10 9 8 7 6 5 4 3 2 1

for suzan & sabrine

contents

publisher's note

I know everytime I read a woman's writing that touches me, I am that much stronger and firmer in believing I could make this world better, not just through my writing but through my activism and just by being me. If other people can do that for me then I know I can do that for people. (Suheir Hammad: Guava Shakti, 1995)

It was on a rainy spring day, surrounded by politically vibrant CUNY students at a rally in 1995 that I met Suheir Hammad. I was 20 years old and angry about the tuition hikes. I heard someone say "Suheir will speak from SLAM" and I became curious hearing a familial name. Her distinctly powerful voice beamed right through us as she rallied unity and change. I followed that voice to the podium and lucky for me she was wearing a long skirt. I was able to reach over (I am very short you see) and tugged on her skirt. She tried to kick me off, but I persisted and in case she thought I was some pervert I called out "Hey! I want to interview you for my women's magazine. Let's be friends!" She turned around—whether she heard me over the chanting CUNY students is not clear—but she smiled and came down to shake my hand. She agreed to be interviewed for Guava Shakti: Voices of Women of Color, a literary magazine that some friends and I had established at Brooklyn College.

Later that month, I took a long winding train ride with her from Williamsburg (pre-hipster years) to accompany her as she delivered her photos to Harlem River Press in SOHO. Along the way, I tape recorded her thoughts on being a poet, a Palestinian, and a woman raised in Brooklyn. I remember that cold winter day in what should have been spring. And I remember Suheir tall, in a mango colored blouse, and with all her rich curls cut off. I was her shadow at the publisher's office and eavesdropped on their discussion about cover design, font and her author's photo.

Who would have believed the voice from the future, if it had said to me then that 15 years later, I would launch a press and reprint this book, this very book that helped develop my spine as a poet and as a woman. I am blessed by the circularity of the universe. Thank you Suheir for your words and your friendship.

–Zohra Saed
Brooklyn, 2010

author's preface (2009)

these poems, written through the unease of growing up, have taken on and discarded meanings in time. writing them, dreaming and breathing them, felt as natural as anything could. the ways a poem formed over months, rolling a knot in my belly over and again until it untied itself onto the page. a new embroidery, stitched in june jordan's dark - the things i thought. never did i think the poems would travel so far, and take me along for a ride stranger and more graceful than a refugee's fairy tale.

i failed at most things in order to write these poems. i often failed at writing the poems. the crash and burn attempts helped clear my vision, to aim better. i wasn't officially studying poetry - how could you do that? - but i read, and i felt there was something in the craft that translated into a sort of freedom for the poet as well as for me, the reader.

every plane of my life i offered to poetry to make sense of.

uhmm...poems don't make sense.
you learn that too.
the poems teach you.
poems have their own lives.
poems are reason and cause.
poems alchemize pain.
poems become markers of time while living outside it.
poems are story, and people are story.

i'm thankful to upset, rob and zohra, for the unconditional.

after many moons of being out of print, poets and teachers are making the book available, again.

it was glen thompson, who first published bpbb, and who proposed the title of the collection, which was an assortment of word processed pages gathered from under my mattress, straightened out and put in the order you have in your hands. i am ever thankful and offer cool water to glen, for his belief, vision and heart.

all the original acknowledgments stand, and many more have been relayed to good folk along the way.

poems are family.

i am grateful for my family and those we come from, each a poem, and a reflection of each.

and to you, there is a country in your heart where story lives and poem comes from.
no one can occupy it.

s.
jersey city/oakland/jerusalem 2009

author's preface (1996)

I was born a Black woman
and now
I am become a Palestinian
against the relentless laughter of evil
there is less and less living room
and where are my loved ones?

It is time to make our way home

–from "Moving Towards Home" by June Jordan

Home is within me. I carry everyone and everything I am with me wherever I go. Use my history as the road in front of me, the land beneath me. Paths are many, but essence is one and eternal.

Language is power, politics. Words can be, as Piri Thomas says, bullets or butterflies. Labels can be empowering or threatening, self-defined or imposed. And in reality, even self-defined labels can be oppressive, limiting. We don't live in a stagnant world. My generation has seen many changes involving technology, environment, and ideology. Yet, with all the changes and upheavals, life basically stays the same. People love, hate, kill, and die. People sing, dance and write.

Why do I write? cause I have to. cause my voice, in all it's dialects, has been silenced too long. cause women are still abused as naturally as breath. Peoples are still without land. Slavery exists, hunger persists and mothers cry. My mother cries. Those are reasons enough, but there are so many more. I'm not here to make anyone comfortable, least of all myself. Just as I try to expand and sharpen my craft I push and challenge myself. With words, labels, and definitions.

There are many usages of the word "Black":

Black   like the coal diamonds are birthed from
like the dark matter of the universe
the Black September massacre of Palestinians
the Arabic expression "to blacken your face"
meaning to shame

Black   like opposite of white
the other
Indians in England, Africans in America,
Algerians in France and Palestinians in Israel
the shvartza labor of cleaning toilets and
picking garbage

Black   like the genius of Stevie, Zora and Abdel-Haleem
relative purity
like the face of God
the face of your grandmother

Choose as many definitions as you want. Make up your own, and get comfortable in it. But use it responsibly, consciously. Have respect for the energy behind words. The history behind labels. Never let them be chosen for you. I decide what it means to be me, here and now. No one else can. I remember times of crazy self-doubt in my life. Not knowing who I was, what I was about, and getting no help from anyone on my questions and feelings. But we're never alone, and I always eventually turned to see my ancestors by my side. See my grandmothers' solar faces.

No matter how much we'd like to make people feel at ease and safe around us, we gotta be for real. We need to own our definitions and live by them. We need not be afraid to adapt or change them when necessary. Borders are manmade, and I refuse to respect them unless I have a say in their formation. Besides, call Spirit what you want, essence is one and eternal.

The last stanza in June Jordan's "Moving Towards Home" changed my life. I remember feeling validated by her statement. She dared speak of transformation, of re-birth, of a deep understanding of humanity. The essence of being Spirit, something no label can touch.

Some of the poems in this volume are four years old. The last one, "Broken and Beirut,"came much later. All of them carry history and emotion. Some were mad cool to write. Others were painful and healing. None of them are pieces that I could write now, cause I'm no longer living in those spaces. But they're still real and breathing, cause those spaces are within me. The road I've traveled, the land beneath my feet. I make my own way home.

–Suheir Hammad
Brooklyn, June 1996

introduction

In 1996 Suheir Hammad whittled the distance between Brooklyn and Palestine into 82 pages. For those of us who hadn't yet sewn the two together into a single sentence, Hammad took a 5,678 mile trail of exile and committed it to paper. It was an act solidified publicly with the first printing of this book, *Born Palestinian, Born Black*, written in the language of her childhood as drawn from a collective memory; set to the cadence of North American resistance that finds footing in Crazy Horse, Malcolm X, and Audre Lorde, with an urban experience informed by rural tact. Hammad considered the time and space of an inherited longing, and for everyone outside of the Palestinian-Israeli conversation, she drew a door on our page and unlocked it with her pen and used her voice to push it open.

What we find to be genuine in the best of these poems is testament to an intimate act: that Hammad's heart has pumped the same blood that you find coursing here. Her fingertips have shaped and caressed these intonations, have gathered what they could of embers from a blaze that still pulsates its heat on Sheepshead Bay sidewalks, in the drivers' seats of midtown Taxis, and in strollers pushed by light veiled women in Queens; a heat that is at once a dry sunray and a cool that is a twilight blanket cast over the crescent moon.

Hammad has drawn a map full of dots we still take pleasure in connecting. She reminds us that North Africa is indeed Africa: Cairo, Morocco, Tangiers—each African. Lest you forget, Hammad reminds us the distance between millenary African Cities and a Palestinian-Israeli conflict, the distance between Cairo and Jerusalem, is only 265 miles—closer than Los Angeles to San

Francisco; closer than Manhattan to Washington D.C.; that Jordan is only set apart from the African continent by the Sinai Peninsula; that the Red Sea doesn't make so much of a difference in this respect, since it is crossed by the dust of footprints and the wet of tears, since without the wind's help ululation reaches from one side of the Suez to the other. Hammad lends voice to such testament, and she does so in a thoroughly Brooklyn accent.

She is the walking version of this book, having moved on some years later to leave these poems as a record of her past, a sort of *Exhibit A* in an argument that she has shaped now for over a decade, securing her link to people in a variety of struggles the world over, and all the while maintaining the crucial, intimate role of poetry in expressing such struggles.

Just 23 years old when *Born Palestinian, Born Black* was published, we've since grown to expect much from her, a new perspective, naturally more mature and informed. Yet this book has not changed. To read *Born Palestinian, Born Black* today is to encounter a very young poet grappling with a variety of themes that will take a lifetime to unravel. The Israeli-Palestinian question is still a complex maze the exit of which none have found. For a 20 year old daughter of refugees to consider a plight to which she is inextricably linked, without the trauma of primary experience, but with the observations of a first-hand witness to its longing, rage, and injustice, is to read the poetry of a young woman struggling to understand her place adrift in what often feels like an uncontrollable current. From her vista in mid 90's New York, at the tail end of the crack era, after a childhood of equal parts hip hop and American tampering in world affairs, Hammad's resulting work springs from hurt, from a sense of despair, and from an incorrigible will toward improvement.

Some readers may have to take a few extra steps in accepting the validity of the younger Hammad's perspective. Her use of a black vernacular may still challenge readers whose categorization of ethnicity divides one slang from another according to pre hip hop notions of legacy and cultural property. But it is precisely here, in the world of language, not politics, that Hammad is successful in expressing herself through the poem. Hers is an engaging language that communicates the dilemma of homeland and exile. It is exactly when the young Hammad was most meditative that she was (and remains) most in control within these poems. This is her success: that she is honest with us, that she is most at home with herself on the Lexington avenue line between Brooklyn and Hunter College; that the speed of her passage through New York intersections births the cadences of her verse while her family legacy provides detailed pronunciation to its sensuality. Years later, she has leapt from page to stage to screen, carrying through each transition the authenticity of her emotional connection to content and her moral commitment to thoughtful justice.

Here is someone who is working her world out from the swirl of visceral experience and onto the open memory of the page in ways that can be criticized, of course, but more importantly in a manner that provides a record of sentiment by which the poet's progress can be measured against the social progress (or lack thereof) to which these poems speak.

Years after its original publication, no ground has been made in securing a peaceful middle east, no ground has been measured in improving the general quality of inner city education, and we remain hungry for progress in the dearest of our social circles, much less the least revered. Despite these shortcomings—as well as because of them—the poet has matured, has dedicated herself to her art more deeply and with greater complexity than ever.

Hammad's work—whether writing, performing, or acting—is a poetry of sensuality, reminding us that pain too is sensual, and like us, these poems are hurting, healing, and living things. So here, in celebration of our common living, let's mark a change: one in which introductions to books of poetry are not by elders, or critics, or even peers, but by witnesses to the impact a poem has had on the world to which it is addressed. There are few of our generation who've made such a sizeable public inroad with their poems over the last decade. Suheir Hammad is one. High school girls know her earliest words by heart. They have read her and felt her and found her sentiments in harmony with their own, and in doing so, have arranged their own words in dialogue with those you will find in these pages. Over the past generation, in Union Square poetry workshops, on HBO television specials, at open mics along the Lower East Side, new poets have sewn Suheir Hammad into their language. This reprinting of *Born Palestinian, Born Black* is in large part meant for the young whose pens will draw from the deepest of inkwells, beginning with Hammad to dip into that well again, to dive headlong into Darwish, Fadwa, and Baldwin; into Audre Lourde, Madhubuti and Rumi—to reach the oldest prophets, their suras and psalms, to reach for sense in our modern mosaic of disaccord, to understand, as Suheir Hammad, that poetry too quenches our thirst.

–Marco Villalobos
Los Angeles, November 2008

born palestinian,
born black

dedication

his name could've been·
ahmad   mustafa   jihad
could've been
mohammad   yousef   hatem
his name was hammad

standing on a mountaintop in jordan
looking over the vast sea

saw the land his people had come from
land of figs and olive trees
what should've been his *phalesteen*

it was close   god it was
so close and
forbidden to him
him the son of the land

his love for phalesteen so fierce
he could've swam there
so light   with such heavy longing
he could've flown there

swore he could smell the ripe olives

closing his eyes
wondered what it would've been like if
we'd been left alone
he'd be with his family
rejoicing a wedding instead of
mourning another death
he'd go to school and write
poetry about the sky   the sun   love
he'd sleep in a bed
in a house
not on floors of tents

he wouldn't cry
no one would cry
only tears of joy shed
in phalesteen

slowly   in pain
opens his eyes
the sea telling him of tears already shed
"our mothers cry enough to fill a million seas"
looking down he aint carrying
books of poetry
but a knife and small pistol

thinks of death and welcomes it
wondering how many days
he's got left
his thoughts not suicidal
thoughts of survival

his fifteen years of life wasted
worrying about eating   feeding his belly
but his mind is hungry   pride starving
he's got to feed to stay alive
his enemies' blood
the only nourishment needed

repelled by the extent of his hatred
feels unhuman thinking evil thoughts
but   his enemies never
believed he was human

he'd prove them wrong
his warm human blood would
fertilize the soil of *phalesteen*

his heart transcending his body
he vowed to return to *phalesteen*
bil roh   *bil dem*
with his life   with his blood

three years later   he was shot
and killed by israeli soldiers
his blood never reached the soil of no palestine
his body never reached home

five years later
his niece travels far
to sit on that same mountaintop
sees palestine over the sea
feels her uncle's heart join hers
thinks of exchanging her books and pencils
for a knife   a small pistol

she vows she'd return to phalesteen
ib rohi   *ib demi*
with my life   with my blood

i close my eyes
and smell the ripe olives

blood stitched time

our kafiyes out of fashion
the stories stitched into them
unraveling round our necks

and now
we've achieved nobel
world peace a noble and worthy cause
we've thank youd thank youd thank youd
those who've denied our humanity eternally
and warmed our bitten hands with
those of our murderers

an eye for an eye
          and when our eyes
               long since bombed out
               are swallowed as olive pits
the whole world is blind
we screamed   our
throats shredded to pieces of meat
thrown to hungry wolves in violent heat

i am the mother
no longer willing to sacrifice sons
to wars of men and
gods of war   i
mother refuse to lose
more daughters to sons gone crazy
watching kids get bombed and blown
into bits of brain and bone

i am the father
          lost his daughters to refugee insanity
the daughter of landless orphans
          child of impotent dreams

and now
kissers of earth   lovers of night
people of god   victims of survival
we understand
stand under the strain of false peace jammed up hopes
we speak with dried olive branches
caught in chests

we call back to the *phalesteen*
of folk songs and village dances
the *phalesteen* of martyrs and their mothers
the *phalesteen* bulldozed over in beirut
whose mouth was jammed silent
with food stamps in brooklyn

now that we've visited the white house
where is the living room jordan spoke of
who holds the key to our house
who lives in our house

now
i am the daughter
coughing up the olive branch
the son rebuilding a nation
the father rebuilding himself
i am the mother
stitching our stories into kafiyes
stitched into our land
of tears and blood
with years and love

i stitch the story
phalesteen
into a kafiye
never to unravel

taxi

i

urban warrior   i think we're
too used to bottled water and soft ass wipes
street soldier not gettin taxis and little white ladies
claspin purses aint all it's about

ii

in my father's city
there's a baby girl
whose beautiful brown eye
(centuries ago inspired poetry)
was eaten out by a fat zionist rat

140 miles of 850,000 souls   gaza
stripped of humanity
the most people in the tiniest place anywhere
tired people with no place everywhere
open sewers carry the sweat of occupation into
the swollen bellies of babies

refugee camps that make you long for
the projects   these kids grow up bad angry murderous
justified   camps are burstin with pictures of
murdered children of fire swimmin
in the tears of a nation   this aint no
boy scout trip this is the real deal   hell
on earth   what it's about

little boys get arrested for thinkin
rocks at armed mercenaries   little boys
get their tender flesh singed with burnin
cigarettes   their heads smothered in piss soaked hoods
fingers cut off as though they were medallions   teeth
broken as though they were powder

pen tubes inserted into penises of little boys
til they confess they were born *phalestini*
confess they were born free

did i turn your stomach?
least i didn't turn your insides to confetti
with a u.s. made machete up your pussy
rape you with my machine gun down your throat
gun point your father to molest
you in front of my army   prostitute your essence
til you confess you were born *phalestinian*
confess you would die the way
you were born   free

closed universities and open prisons
curfews and house demolitions
the israeli flag is red white and blue too
this red drips from billy clubs and soldiers boots
this red soaks the faces of mournin mothers
losin more sons to american tax dollars

iii

corner chaplain slow down
your bible and quran talk for a second
the land jesus was born in is bein crucified
the land of milk and honey is drownin in blood
the devil is alive overseas   alive and kickin
the hell outta palestine

conscious comrade
there's a place uglier than uptown's slum
where the people are just as beautiful
strugglin sister
there's a *debke* beat funky as p.e.'s riff
signalin revolution liberation and freedom

so when we're vibin on the pale
evil of welfare and crack   know i'm
across the street and across the sea   so when
we're combatin cops and prisons   know there are prisons
like ansar iii   nazis wouldn't touch pigs wouldn't visit
so when we read baraka and listen to malcolm
let's read darwish and keep on
listenin to malcolm

so when you call me sista
ask after our family
this shit is about more
than the newest gear and
the biggest booty
it's bigger than
our hoods and our heads
it aint all about this poem
and it aint all about
taxis
and little white women

mariposa

my posse & me
would dance da dance of da flamenco flamingo
in our fresh filas
around da flames of wet food stamps

as bleached blonde brunettes
w/burn scars on dare necks
prepared sad salads dressed
w/massala & salsa rhythms
& peppered w/ still hot bullets shot
through da hands of frustrated boys
who shoulda been home for dinner awready

as voltron   da fierce drag queen on acid
captivated us w/ cartoon vodou
& pacman had us spendin cash money on
cereals w.i.c. wouldn't cover
bubble gum wrappers w/ our fortunes on dem
were cast into wings & stapled to our backs

my posse & me
silenced da sirens & da screams & da sadness
w/ da speed of our flight

all we heard was da rap of da angels
as we singed our antennas w/ da
hungry heat of our heavens

had to get away
my posse took to flight
to get away from
rulin roaches
pure poverty
leach landlords
hungry homes

some of dem laid w/ anyone
just to get out of dare tight ass jeans
& sad ass lives
others fought dare way into enemy territory
always with attitude & razor ready
flyin away from nightmares of strangers touchin em
& generic cereal
white heroes
eulogizin education
to get away from beatins by daddy &
questions from welfare
some wrote lyrics & poems
most got high da popular road
smokin & shootin away dare
checks
cash
kids
youth

our wings w/ all
the colors of da ghetto were
stretched to da gods of gold children
for relief from da greed & da greasy & da green
patterned w/ loud happy garish motifs
our wings flew over our
sneakered feet

sad & weighed down w/ cheap jewelry and
cheaper excuses
we've forgotten we knew how to fly

staplin our wings
cause day got in da way of walkin
we've forgotten how to fly

suicide watch

aint no time for thoughts of suicide
we gotsta entertain homicide

but billboards bombard us
with calvin klein crotches & butt cracks
bag of crack   cracked bodies   & body bags

colored girls commit suicide
buying ugly lies & no lye straight &
straight nose lies
thinkin the rainbow aint enuf
        anyway the rainbow was a slave ship

let it rain the kind that got no end
no rainbows & no green pot of gold
wash them thoughts out of your (fried) head
        of glocs & pops against your brotha
        of bitch & whore against your sista

time to dust this dirt off our brains
& stop sniffin it up our noses
tyin our own nooses
with drivebys & daddy's bye-byes
with beat up women & gun sportin children

let it rain the wrath of crazy horse
that manic native in the sky
let it flood with the sweat of shaka zulu
with holy water from some frustrated vodou
cleanse your eyes of blonde & blue
purify your spirit from red white and blue

enough of this
colonial commercialization of ancient civilzations
right when we need to rebuild nations

get offa this suicide watch we on
we need to watch our backs
release earth's wrath
on those who sin against humanity
who place a baby's health underneath vanity
those who trade wealth for our sanity

but tv infects us with v.d. & van damme
and damming programming
programs of purple gay dinosaurs
gettin us up the butt while we
got each other by the throats
enough of this
kill barney

kill barney & ronald mcdonald
& beaver & gilligan too
cook up lambchop & serve his ass as stew
quiet that white boy in the white house
while you at it
clog his saxophone with old english
& country club &
make him play his soul til
he admit   damn it taste like shit

o.d. the tv & rip up the radio
less it plays only trane & marley & p.e.
kill the evil
& serve mankind
kill the evil &
service your humanity

we gotsta
gotta get off this suicide watch we on
& smell out the real enemy

one stop (hebron revisited)

i wish i woulda
woulda caught you on the train
on an empty car into flatbush

woulda reached into the conductor's booth
grabbed an *intifada* stone and
crushed your skull
to dig up your thoughts and
burn them up

woulda glued on some fake nails
to carve out your green heart
all your devious juices squirting out
and thrown it on the tracks

woulda
opened my blouse
so you coulda
opened your pants
woulda stomped on your slimy flesh til
you were underground
with the rats
with the rats gagging on you

woulda taken your rabid star of david
stabbed you in the gut
til your screams were heard bouncing
off the wailing wall
moses woulda heard you scream

woulda grabbed that damn book that
entitles you to murder
cause you were favored
to   destined to   chosen to
claim my land
damn god aint no real estate agent

woulda ripped the pages into a cross
crucified your ass
right there on church ave

woulda wrapped that stethoscope round your neck
til your eyes rolled under my feet
stompin to my *debke* beat

woulda waited til you were finished
with your evil ablutions
blasphemous prayers
and shot you right between the eyes
so i coulda
watched you die

cause it aint kosher
brooklyn boy
to kill the kneeling in prayer
aint kosher to cook the flesh of palestine in
ramadan blood
no it aint
kosher

you
coulda been messiah
chosen to breathe a sigh of relief
with every fallen palestinian
brother and sister
so you could sit down at your
pass-us-over cedar
aint kosher
brooklyn boy

but the spirit has
let me know
your gonna get yours

cause the train you on got
one stop
the train you on got only one stop
and im'a be there when
you get off

scarlet rain

mama stop cryin over
scarlet o'hara
save your tears your
people need them to
water soil of uprooted olive trees
stop sobbin over that
confederate curtain wearin slave owner
believe me she
don't give a damn

you cry enough for
that 21 year old palestinain youth
parents watched him bleed to death in 3 slow hours
from a settler's bullet   and army imposed curfew
your tears could have clotted his blood

where were your sad sad sighs
when our kids were bein targeted
through school yard fences or
when uzis raped little girls til they collaborated with
the promise of an occupied
life as a reward

does that old southern charm really
get to you in a
technicolor kinda way
the west bank just can't
is rhett butler all that smoother
than the tens of thousands of our men who
suffer unrequited love due to
incarceration   death   and other
casualties of war

did miss scarlet survive
cigarette burns and
slash whippins

her endearin plantation demolished within
an hour's notice
did that land even belong to her through
any decent notion of ancestry

stop your snivelin and sniffin up
mistress's ballgown
it's funky as hell down there
there's a reason everything burned down

decades after gas grenades have bombed
out your eyes
you wipe your tears with
petticoats and pinafores
                                        that insult your humanity
even more

we got all the melodrama we
can deal with
rubber bullets empty hopes   deportations   broken bones
45 years beyond despair
i see why you wanna cry

enough tears mama
enough   cause your tears
won't clot any blood

save those deep brown eyes
from any more rain
stop cryin mama
let miss scarlet
burn in hell

argela remembrance

smoking the water pipe
pass the *argela*
    head tipped down
to my father
inhaling strawberry tobacco
exhaling mediterranean breezes
mid east sighs
him telling me

        we are a people
      stood on the edge of the sea
   asked her to kiss our toes goodnight
     she kissed them goodbye
       we departed
    with those sea and hibiscus kisses
   yellow hibiscus kisses shadowing
     our path goodbye

  we read futures in search of our past
    in coffee grinds and tea leaves
    in upturned hands grasping
       for prayer

      we are a people
   name our sons after prophets
    daughters after midwives
    eat with upturned hands
   plant plastic potted plants
   in suffocating apartments
    tiny brooklyn style
  in memory of the soil once
    laid under our nails
   collect sea shells in
  honor of goodnight kisses

    we call ourselves the east
  and face each other when we pray

inhaling strawberries through argelas
we've become a people of
living room politics and tobacco
stained teeth   painfully
reminding each other
reciting quranic verse and
urn kolthom scripture
of how jasmine can
fill your head on a clear night and
mint tea dawned you to morning

my father passes the water pipe
        head tipped down
to suheir
blowing out a puff of
sweet smoke
he tells her

                        baba
        we once stood on the edge of our sea
                but they made us leave

i try to stop his crying
sea foam escaping his eyes

the necklace

... a form of execution in which a crowd pinions the prey
inside a tire, douses it with gasoline and turns the victim into
a horrible flaming scarecrow.
—*The New York Times Magazine* (May 14, 1995)

survivors of horror
victims of never again victims

before 1948 fifty-six
arab towns sighed breath in
the ramleh sub-district of palestine
within a year of israel's birth
bastard birth
all fifty-six were demolished
two cities allowed a weak
palestinian presence

my father from
one citylydd
gifted my mother   from ramleh
the other
a necklace for their engagement
her gazelle neck wore it
perfectly even as
it seared her skin
burned her breast

the necklace
diamonds of south african rock
piercing shine caught in eyes
charred bone of der yessin's massacre
carried memories of my grandfather's
chocolate and nuts shop

amber-caught tears clasped the back

weight of the necklace laid
heavy against her belly
my mother pregnant knelt
to clean floors of her refugee home
inside womb i could
hear jangle of beads
promise me a life of
palestinian frustration
palestinian dreams
tellin me stories of these two
soul surviving villages

at birth
the necklace tangled
in my curly hair
welcomed me into
man's world of liquor and war
my mama she
tightened it round her neck
so i baby
wouldn't mess with it

survivors of victims
my father gifted my mother
a necklace
he strung on it jewels he'd seen
young men mauled by army dogs
rifles ripped through young girls
families shot in the back outside
generational homes entire
families burned to bones

the circle unbroken
my mother not only wore this necklace
she worked it
with every beating and
baby feeding

names of the murdered
embedded in beads
embedded in her marriage bed

the marriage of *lydd* and *ramleh*
marriage of *mohammad* and *muntaha*

what survivors of struggle do
to one another
my parents later
gifted the necklace into three
one for suheir
one for suzan
one for sabrine

children of stone

now that our soil has become co-conspirator
eating up our dreams and dusty tears
bearing the fruit of our horrors
in orange navels
rooting us yet stronger
firmer to our ancestors' bones

we ask

when did stones
become the comrades of sunken boys
who utilize rubber bullets and empty shells
as toys
?

when did stones
become the confidants of young girls
whose clothes and pride
across the river were hurled
?

when war smoked
his way into our collective dream
were we awake
?

or
did the morningstar
dawn on us
to the rhythmless din of rape
?

yo baby yo

1. scenario

door knocker earrings		drug dealin earnins
gucci leather		polo sweater
gold tooth front	&	frontin with a 40
belt by fendi		shoes by nike
crotch grab bin		5-0 clockin
smokin blunts		on the hunt
twistin the cap		twistin nappppy hair
	into knots	
shirts by tommy		jeans by perry

what have you done for this sista lately?

2. existence

poppin that yo baby yo
yo baby yo?
me to turn around you expect after
you show me no kind of respect?

the sneakers you wearin cost more than
the soul you sold to pay for them?

the sherling you sportin worth more than
our children goin hungry
so you could go clubbin?

slicin each other up over a dirty look
go ahead   act like you look
people you can buy are
never worth the cash or
the time

3. scenario

name plate
slathered in vaseline
drinkin coolers of wine
gloc cleaned and shined
sippin warm black cherry
wallet by coach

jail bait
bottle pumpin curl sheen
lips don't touch swine
herbal buzz on the mind
bullet wounds honor you carry
pimp style approach

yo baby yo
yo brotha yo
them gold chains
are tighter than you think

fly away

for Kevin

young brother man
       wanna fly
in the u.s. air force
says it's better than bein high
       and forced
into the back of a police car
he gonna go far

and away
from the shootins   the drugs   and the street
       be up in the air
yeah   a techno pegasus with sneakered feet

out my mouth trail the places
america's military has visited
       saigon   beirut   greneda
out his mouth trail the faces
       the young dark faces
       the sad scarred faces
american society has enlisted
in the struggle for existence
       shaquan   jesus   t'kalla

young brother don't wanna
hear bout nuclear bombs and
world domination
       he's gotta support his moms
       give up donations
       for the next funeral
someone else's child died too soon
       nurse his uncle
       keep his sister outta trouble
all while watchin his back
you never know who's carryin a piece

my words of
revolution and peace
can't get through his cloud
that's where he wanna be up
in the sky with
the birds and the unicorns
and the angels

i say it's dangerous up
there too   never
know when you'll get shot
when the war is lost
when the engine will die
what if you have to kill people

might as well stay in the city

he explains
my words
of revolution and peace
don't sound so real and cool
cause he's dealin with
a different kinda fear
at least up in the sky
you got an
eject button

aint nothin like that down here

silence

i wonder what he
heard as he ran
wonder what he
thought as the
            american bullets
flew from
            israeli hands
through
            god's air
to murder another
one of freedom's sons

he didn't look back

did he hear the loud strong
voices of our women
voices so clear
songs so sad   so beautiful
strained   drained
by years of crying
(singing) *Ishad ya ãlam alena wa ã Beirut*
              Ishad il hãrb il shabiyeh
              (Bear witness world to us and to Beirut
              Bear witness to the War of Liberation)

did he hear the
angels who'd proclaimed the birth
of jesus in that same land
angels singing songs of
heaven   angels who arose from
the earth after dying
too young in the
name of palestine

ran so fast
as his brown feet
touched loved   touched loved
the brown earth
did he hear his
mama singing him
to sleep

he had lived with his eyes

seen so much
palestine occupied   freedom denied   my people's genocide
seen with his eyes
felt with his heart
struggle of life under
army boots

palestine alive
(singing) *Wa men ma shaf bil ghorban ya Beirut*
          Āman āyoon Amreeciya
          (And those who don't see through the sieve
          Are blinded by American eyes)

not been blinded by
american eyes
saw it all and he
knew   what did he
hear as he ran

so used to running
we are   it seems
we palestinians are always running

where do we go
never looking back
Ishad ya alam alene wa a Beirut
(Bear witness world to us and to Beirut)
                    they warned him to stop

called out in the name of
democracy and violence
called out in the tongue
of the ancients to
halt his running

they fired their
american made bullets
did he hear them
from israeli hands
through god's air
into palestine's son
(singing)

they labeled it
an accidental
but necessary death
when discovered this
son of palestine
had been born
deaf
(singing)
Wa men ma shaf bil ghorban ya Beirut
Ãman ãyoon Amreeciya

dead woman

tradition says you can tell a dead woman by the way she walks
going no where a little
too fast
the way her eyes
black and blue
tear and dry

wearing fragrance heavy
to hide the smell of blood
violent and dried on
her thigh

you can hear the death of a woman
in her screams against the sky
muffled muted and mutated

made-up to conceal her death
taste the tired in her bones bruises
on her back lashes
in her smile

you can smell the death of a woman
on her sister's breath
as the story of her people's
sad laughter is told

dead woman   i am

murdered at birth
born to a people years dead
before i inhaled a
struggled breath

won't live until
we once again
taste our breath as sacred

until we exhale
this struggled air
to rebuild our
demolished homes   souls
return to our soil

i am a dead woman
until we inhale our collective
breath healing
our pierced lungs
refilling our hardened hearts

won't breathe
will not breathe
unless my very breath
is a sacred
act of prayer

99 cent lipstick

there is out there
a deep dark   void sucking
in my   deep   dark people

afraid i
hid behind cheap red
99 cent lipstick
dull 12 kt doorknocker earrings

fearful   abused anger as
my primary language
labeled myself a bitch
before anyone else could

afraid of dying young
we shot each other up
when we weren't shooting up
hiding behind greasy
guns and dirty needles

we became each other's
niggas and hoes
so we wouldn't belong to anyone else
just so we could belong to ourselves

for arthur at 17
young black male in jail
he became a breathing statistic
for richie at 16
by junior year
his hand was forever bent
frozen around a fantasy 40

we sliced our pain into
each other's faces with
rusty blades hid
our fear behind dirty
looks and attitude
cool was what we ate
tough was what we talked
concealing our hungry
fragile youth beneath
hunched shoulders and
bad posture

for shelley
a baby at 11 she was
pregnant at her grade school graduation
for sha
so angry at america's god
at 16 he became his own

our fear was stronger than
that cheap red lipstick that
bled on me
my people have bled on me

the horror of our situation hit
us right in the face   right into
our gold tooth fronts and
dirty looks

afraid we hid behind our
curls   curses   crosses

for jason
his rap poetry more eloquent than any shakespeare
for mike
urban warrior with heart of a country mouse

we pointed guns bought with dirty
food stamps at each other
shot bullets of frustration through
each other
that's right we killed each other
we killed each other with our
*a*ttitudes   *b*ullets   *c*rosses   *d*irty looks

            for junior shot to death at 12
        by his 15 year old drug dealing bosses
            he spent their money to buy candy

we killed each other with
a fear that wasn't even ours
a cheap red horror that was
older than our tired youth

        for suzan   sabrine   sameeh   omar
    cause there are nights when i'm still afraid
            for us

    this fear don't even belong to us

brown bread hero

may i have a vegetable hero?
no white
rye or wheat
      brown
yeah   a brown bread hero
brown
born and bred

no mayonnaise thank you
never liked it as much as
mustard   i'll take spicy yellow or
sweet brown mustard over
bland fatty white mayo
anyday

no cheese please
cheese is to the west
the spice of the east
why smother in cheese
when i can enhance
spice dance
with tumeric   sumac or curry
no mucous building cheese on my hero

vegetables of the brown earth
between two layers of brown bread
no flesh of creatures
no white bread
no salt   no sauce
thank you

a brown bread hero
brown born and bred
white has never been
my hero

delicious

why is it men
describe our colors
as edible
?

chocolate skinned
sweet honey shade
cafe au lait   delicious
olive (an acquired taste)
peaches and cream
brown sugar

is it
because they are
always ever
so ready to

eat us
?

tabla tears

i wear kohl round my eyes
stares round my hips
eyes smother and cover
my sway as i
swing their worries
away and desire pierces
my navel

in drunken tears i see
beirut destruction   broken
boricua hunger bosnian
ashes brooklyn despair

they don't bother to
look in my eyes   ever

only in this night
here between my breasts and
round my waist in the
arch of my wrist and the
stretch of my neck
i command

ears fill with the
blood of my dance
they can't hear the
tabla   conga   percussion or
know the difference

what difference
i take stories of
exile   loneliness   want
and string them through
my hair braid fear
machismo   fantasies   horrors
round my thigh and up
my spine

only here in this night
i'm not mama or whore
mouths forget the spitting
curses of the day gone
hands caress empty glasses
forget the fists flown into faces

lust   longing   love
pierce my left lung as
i breathe in the
tabla's air   close my
eyes to drunken tears of
grown men and dance their stares and
desires away

good word

begged mohammad for his help
he let me know he don't deal
with no whores told him i was a virgin
but you got the heart of a whore   he said

begged solomon to put in a good word with fate
he said i'd have to marry him
replied i was saving myself for another prophet
too bad he don't deal with no virgins

on my knees i pleaded to jesus
"sorry   i only deal with virgins or whores"
was born a virgin and plan to be a whore   i promised
called over his shoulder "already got my two marys"

buddha wasn't down with my troubles
he couldn't understand my intimacy problems
osiris couldn't hang cause
my temple didn't hang right
jehovah wasn't even trying to hear me
too far back on line
jah told me to smoke my trials away
my lungs too small for his divine high

my knees bloody
from kneeling forever
pages of all the holy books stained my hands red
my eyes burned from the incense in all those temples
blood of all the holy wars stained my hands red
the prayer rugs frayed and soiled
prayer beads loose on the floor
slipping me up

no communion   baptism   nile libation
aint no ritual around to cleanse me of
these demands

the prophets gotta pay the rent
gotta get off too
the messengers gotta do what they
gotta do   they gotta
pimp and scheme
just like we do
then they come to me
asking for a good word

may i take your order?

i'm the main dish
walkin down the street
my face a menu
of first world delicacies
olive skin   almond eyes   bitter tongue
& my ears burnin w/ comments days beyond
rude   crude   & lewd
men suck my titties in
eyes poppin out big business heads
lickin their lips against
my thighs like i was some
cafe au lait ice cream

i must look spicy & exotic
cause he's wonderin if i sell
my curry pussy
or lend it free
& if i'm as finger lickin good
as the liver his mama used to
stew   fry   bake
for her little anemic boy

yeah   i'm the
white boy's spam
to be processed   diluted   canned
so his tender digestion can
take it   but i give it a
south of the border tang
w/ jalepeno hips & guacamole looks

he stir fries me w/
questions like
         where you from
brooklyn
i mean originally
yeah   there's no hidin i'm original recipe

from the region of
figs   lentils   &   pomegranates
but he wants to know

can he lick soy sauce
off my body
would i dance my
belly for him
shimmy and shake for his shiny penny
would i suck chocolate offa his
macdaddy macadamia nuts
can he soak me
in falafel oil
& drain milk & honey outta me

my brown eyes remind him
of the expensive chocolates he
used to steal from his mama's purse
except mine refuse to melt

he gets up real close
& wishes he had a dick
for every hole in my body
i say
chiiiiilll
white boy

& just pray for one

exotic

don't wanna be your exotic
      some delicate   fragile colorful bird
      imprisoned   caged
      in a land foreign to the stretch of her wings

don't wanna be your exotic
      women everywhere are just like me
      some taller   darker nicer than me
      but like me but just the same
      women everywhere carry my nose on their faces
      my name on their spirits

don't wanna
      don't seduce yourself with
      my otherness   my hair
      wasn't put on top my head to entice
      you into some mysterious black vodou
      the beat of my lashes against each other
      aint some dark desert beat
      it's just a blink
      get over it

don't wanna be your exotic
      your lovin of my beauty aint more than
      funky fornication   plain pink perversion
      in fact nasty necrophilia
      cause my beauty is dead to you
      i am dead to you

not your
      harem girl   geisha doll   banana picker
      pom pom girl pum pum shorts   coffee maker
      town whore   belly dancer   private dancer
      la malinche   venus hottentot   laundry girl
      your immaculate vessel emasculating princess

don't wanna be
          your erotic
not your exotic

our mothers and their lives of suffer

raised to fetch slippers and brew tea
kill chickens and roast lambs
you scrubbed floors raw
on knees bleeding exhaustion
fed babies and watered plants
you embroidered your dreams
into scarves and veils

married to men you did not know
so how could you love
you learned to love through
your children
their baby whimpers and
nipple sucking

when your land is raped you
thank god you still have husbands
when your husbands are jailed
you thank god for your sons
when your sons are murdered   execution style
you hide your daughters and
when they are found and jailed
you fast til they return
and pray some more and
when they are as their land   raped
you prepare bandages and some
more prayer and when your family
loses all faith you
pray for their souls

half your sons leave   crazy
to be with the enemy's woman
the other half stay   crazy
to take out their hunger
on your daughters

and when we your
daughters say we are
about more than chickens and tea
you ask who do
we think we are
we're no better than you
and you are right

we take your smoldering strength and
maternal love to throw as
stones at mercenaries
use your patience as shields in the nights
your womb   our shelter
your heart   where we bury our dead

you softly recite our poetry
in songs sad and true
fast for our return and
pray for our souls

we mistake your strength
for acquiescence
cause it's brown and quiet

remind us mothers
how you are the ones who
converse daily with ancestors
dialogue with angels
curse the devil
and through your exile
still cook the best okra though
force us to eat it

we   your daughters
        and our men
honor our mothers
and the lives
they survived

we follow the sun each day
     it rises in the east
as you once did
and warms us
as you once did

bleached and bleeding

we bleach our skin
    burn our hair
    flatten our curves

we straighten our nose
    purse our lips
    bite our tongue

we chop off our tongue
    staple our stomach
    sew up our vulva

we stifle our laugh
    shut our mouth

close our eyes
kill our soul

sexless
no voice no soul
we come to you

you molest
you rape
you blame us

we blame ourselves
we hate ourselves
we kill ourselves

you dominate
    detain
you dehumanize

we come to you
tired and poor
bleached and bleeding

we come to you
inhaling your hatred
yearning to breathe
free

you pat us on the head
	bed us for the night
	give us our book of food stamps
	kick us in the belly

ismi

please
learn to pronounce
the name of my spirit
the spirit of my name
correctly

and don't complain
it's too throaty
too deep
too guttural

begin it in your gut
let it tickle the back of your throat
warm under tongue
let it perfume your breath
smooth your lips

and release it
round my hips
clearly

manifest destiny

we four
sitting nursing
plates of rice and beans in a cuban diner
we all should have been other people
with other people

one
who should've been a neo-nazi aryan baby breeder
or a machete wielding man-hating dyke
was a lover of both men and women   girl of riot   and a poet

another
who should've been a witness of jehovah knocking down doors
or a gyrating video hoochie
was a scholar of african glory   lover of knowledge   and a poet

the other
should've been a cold landowning elitist
or a rich corporate robot
was a fighter for independence   lover of an island   and a poet

and me
who should've been a doctor of western medicine
or married   at least engaged   but always obedient
me   searcher of truth   lover of humanity   and a poet

missing my family
who couldn't understand
we four all missing family who wouldn't understand
creating a family
we struggling to understand
we were where we needed to be
we are who we have to be

open poem to those who rather we not read...
or breathe

fascism is in fashion
but we be style
    dressed in sweat danced off taino and arawak bodies
we   children of children exiled from homelands
    descendants of immigrants denied jobs and toilets
carry continents in our eyes
    survivors of the middle passage
we   stand
and demand recognition of our humanity

starving for education
we feed on the love of our people
we flowers
the bloom on amsterdam ave
though pissed on by rich pink dogs
through concrete cracks

we   passion kiss in the backs of police vans
    recite poetry in prison cells
    stained walls in blood tracing brutality
    know the willow she weeps for
we   her jazzy tears taste the fruit of brooklyn trees

fascism is in imperial fashion
but we be style
our tongues   long slashed to keep silence
wear blood jewels
our heads sport civilizations
hips velvet wrapped in music
and you can see the earth running
right under our skin

in a state of police
    cops act as pigs   treat men as dogs
    mothers as whores
the bold youth of a nation hungry and cold
an entire nation of youth   behind bars grown old
the mace and blood did not blind   we
witness and demand a return to humanity

we   braid resistance through our hair
    pierce justice through our ears
    tattoo freedom onto our breasts

the bluesy souls of brown eyed girls
clash with blood on the pale hands of
governments of war
cops who think they're
bluer than they are black
mercenaries sent on a mission to set back
our strength   power love

we be eternal style
while evil wears itself down with
guns   contracts   laws   cash
and rouges it's thin lips with human juice
strained off billy clubs
and tightens it's power tie round necks that
just won't bend
we see the price tag dangling out

the cost is our death and
we refuse to pay

we be political prisoners walking round semi-free
our very breath is a threat
to those who rather we not read
and think   analyze   watch out   and fight back
and be human beings the way we need to be

we wear warrior marks well

fashion is passing
style is everlasting
we

patience

i await you tonight
with my spirit sharp as a blade
ready to slice

i await you in silence
my people's screams & cries of horror
mixing with the sound of crickets

i await you in sunlight
my soul kissed by the warmth
shiny as the blade i carry
i wait in silence

i play with the butterflies
while cleaning my blade
i clean in the rivers
enjoying the fish
while i await you

i await you in the dark
the moon playing a game of
shadows with me
the night flowers opening
while we await you

for these flowers & butterflies
these rivers & this soul
belong to this land
you cannot own them

i await you forever
to laugh at your
official documents, legal treaties

the fish & butterflies & flowers laugh
we laugh at your tanks & bombers
we carry our spirits
sharp as swords
we await you

shoulder to shoulder
our soldiers in the battlefield
our grandparents in their graves
our future in their wombs
shoulder to shoulder
sharp as the tall grass
strong as the morning tide

our dancer's sweat...the dew on the leaves
our mother's cries...the soaring bird above

we await you
know you will come
for it seems your nature
we smell your greed
taste your money
while i crouch in the fields
i wait for you

these fields & shadows
this spirit & life
belong to this land
and you cannot own us

and for you we wait

we spent the fourth of july in bed

even now
young walking girls are exploding legs
stepping on shells of
american hatred left
dug in iraqi soil

even now malaysian girls
must choose between the sex trade and
hunger   young philipinas
go blind constructing the computer discs
poems like this are saved on

ants crawl out of somali eyes
a puerto rican woman goes blind in
an all white prison cell
self-determination her crime
yemeni eyes search out concrete
bodega walls to feed
homesick elders and
beepers and sneakers burst
round brown bed stuy eyes

yeah   the smell of suffer
lingers   even now
lover   as we lay
in amazement and
if baby as you say

my skin is the color of sun
warmed sand   then your
my moonless night and
we the beach
wet   and tidal   all that
good shhhh   wet   yet
as we lay

shrapnel awakens pain on
an island of young paraplegics
courtesy of the 80s gun craze
to our generation violence
isn't a phase   it's the day to day

and though my head is filled
with your sweetness now
this same head knows
nagasaki girls picked maggots out of stomach sores with
    chopsticks
and hiroshima mothers rocked headless babies to sleep
this head knows
phalestini youth maimed absorbing rubber bullets
homes demolished   trees uprooted   roots dispersed

this same head with
all them love songs and
husky whispers knows
our moans come with a history
deeper than groins   our
groans marry a story older
than this lust

as we lay   and love
our touch is not free
it comes with memories
and the reality that even now
food is a luxury
viruses free

limbs mangled hang limp
from fig trees and southern
family tree limbs limp
with the names of the murdered

we baby
look into our browness to
see those who've gone without
knowing this   comfort of entangled legs
foreheads of sweat   heart beats of love and sex

our sighs indeed heavy with
history   destiny   cum   and responsibility
even now   in this heat
on this futon
we are not alone

on this third day of my
seven day candle   the flame
flickers on bodies   on my walls of lavender purple
in the shadows we see goddesses   abandoning children
daughters and their nations getting
raped with big guns by
bastard sons of the earth

even as we lay in
all this good feeling
people lay in dirt   vomit   shit   and blood
and i gotta tell you
that my sincere love   for real
is for my peeps   my family   humanity
love for real   for real freedom
well fed human dignity
for sisters and their lovers

lover even now
i open myself to
share this
i gotta tell you

there aint enough good feeling
to push the pain and awareness out

not enough nothing to
make me forget

and i aint no
woman of steel
it feels needed   this touch   that
kiss   there   that rhythm
needed and wanted   yeah   now

hold me a little while longer
just a bit   just
a bit   cause we
gotta get up soon
come on now baby
we got work to do

broken and beirut

no mistakes made here
these murders are precise
mathematical
these people blown apart   burned alive
flesh and blood all mixed together
a sight no human being can take

and yet we take and take
desensitized to the sacred defamed
witness youth strap 40 lbs of
dynamite to sore bodies cause
we always return to what we know
and if that's war
we return over and over to it
sit at its feet to
remove stone shoes   bones and blues

don't know what to do with visions
of blown up babies   so we
lamé nails and lame tongues
which should protest
love those who cannot
love us   hate ourselves   and become
obsessed with puzzles

shifting through rubble   we ask
where is the head that goes with this 7-year-old shoulder
shattered   this leg looks like it fits with this hip
this dead with that dead   cause they wear twin rings
on bloated purple hands

tired of taking fear and calling it life
being strong and getting
over shit   to prepare for more shit

(when my heart was broken i turned to the only dynamic i knew
more hurtful   my father)

we return to what we know
it's 1996 and beirut all over again
this time the murdered are those who survived the last time
and this time's survivors are preparing for the next time
when fire will rain down on heads bowed in prayer

i want to go home
not only to mama and baba
i want to go home to before me and
pain   bombs and war   before
loveless sex   poetry   and chocolate

i want to remember what i've never lived
a home within me   within us
where honey is offered from my belly
to sweeten babies' breath   make boys moral
and girls strong

want to return to the belly of my honey
and feed myself earth
before 1996   1982   '73   and '48
before tv   race   marriage   and meat

return to what we've forgotten
what hunger has faked
return to the whiteness of black
to the drum   the hum   the sum of my parts
to god   the boiling in my belly
touch it taste   name it and
come back to here

come back   and make no mistake
be precise   get back to work
shifting through the rubble   mathematically
building a new day
with offerings of honey and memory

never forgetting
where we come from
where we've been
and how sweet honey
on the lips of survivors

the gaza suite

gaza

a great miracle happened here
a festival of lights
a casting of lead upon children
an army feasting on epiphany

i know nothing under the sun over the wall no one mentions
some must die wrapped in floral petroleum blanket
no coverage

i have come to every day armageddon
a ladder left unattended
six candles burn down a house
a horse tied to smoke
some must die to send a signal

flat line scream live stream river a memory longer than life spans
the living want to die in their country

no open doors no open seas no open
hands full of heart five daughters wrapped in white

each day jihad
each day faith over fear
each day a mirror of fire
the living want to die with their families

the girl loses limbs her brother gathers arms
some must die for not dying

children on hospital floor mother beside
them the father in shock this is my family
i have failed them this is my family i did
not raise their heads i have buried them
my family what will i do now my family is bread
one fish one people cut into pieces

there is a thirst thefts life
there is a hunger a winter within winter

some must die to bring salvation
i have come to end times always present

the woman lost parents her children and screams
my sister i have lost my sister i want to die
my sister's eyes were honey her voice mine
i can't face this only god only god my sister

medics killed schools hit convoys bombed
the injured are dying the dead are buried in three
hours the people pray together and curse the people
mourn loud and quiet always too loud not enough

some must die because they are the vicinity
some must die because it was written

no army does not apologize has never
apologized authority chases paper assembly
occupation settles deeper

a great miracle here
the living are dying and the dying living

a festival of lights
a strip a land a blaze
the sea a mirror of fire

a casting of lead upon children
their heads roll off their shoulders into streets
their tops spin in hands

an army feasting on epiphany
driving future into history
carrying torches into women

jabaliya

a woman wears a bell carries a light calls searches
through madness of deir yessin calls for rafah for bread
orange peel under nails blue glass under feet gathers
children in zeitoun sitting with dead mothers she unearths
tunnels and buries sun onto trauma a score and a day rings
a bell she is dizzy more than yesterday less than
tomorrow a zig zag back dawaiyma back humming suba

back shatilla back ramleh back jenin back il khalil back il quds
all of it all underground in ancestral chests she rings
a bell promising something she can't see faith is that
faith is this all over the land under the belly
of wind she perfumed the love of a burning sea

concentrating refugee camp
crescent targeted red

a girl's charred cold face dog eaten body
angels rounded into lock down shelled injured shock

weapons for advancing armies clearing forests sprayed onto a city
o sage tree human skin contact explosion these are our children

she chimes through nablus back yaffa backs shot under
spotlight phosphorous murdered libeled public relations

public
relation

a bell fired in jericho rings through blasted windows a woman
carries bones in bags under eyes disbelieving becoming
numb dumbed by numbers front and back gaza onto gaza
for gaza am sorry gaza am sorry she sings for the whole
powerless world her notes pitch perfect the bell a death toll

rafah

there is a music to this all
the din has an order of orders
a human touch behind all arms
all of it manufactured stars above all

something melting a dove molting mourning through dusk

one child after another gathered if possible
washed where possible wrapped there is always cloth
all the while prayed on then pried from the women
always the women in the hot houses of a winter's war
the cameras leave with the men and the bodies always
the women somehow somehow putting tea on fire
gathering the living children if possible
washing them when possible praying on them
through their hair into their palms onto dear life

something fusing into dawn feathers shed eyes

people in a high valence state
that's when breathing feeds burns
that's where settlers take high ground
that's how villages bulldozed betwixt
holidays before your eyes
high violence holy children lamb
an experience no longer inherited
actual
earth in scorched concrete
heart in smoking beat

tel el hawa

what day is it
alkaline of neck alley base
of musk alcohol top note

what the night was like
blooming sky white smoke black out
a dawn flaming life

so long this winter
so cold this shadow
what day is it

a woman dreams a baby years
embroiders wishes names angels
a future onto cloth the people carry her
child shelled streets shaheed

what day is it

a father works hours to bone to feed
seed dress them bless them buries them
his pain a sonic collapse
who can imagine

today the first day
last night the worst night

zeitoun

where from here
a ribbon of land smoking
within the girl's hair smoking
wire wood word smoking
there are bodies here
micro mosaic children
a triptych exile against wall
my dead are rescued
a closing of crossings
a scatter vapor of earth
a trance of metal
where from here

i am all tunnel

afterword

But what does Suheir Hammad *mean* when she says she is "born Black?" Black, in her case, not being mere ethnic marker but a political position in relation to a dominant power structure. As Hammad herself explains in her introduction to this book, the word has numerous historical and political meanings that she embraces, but the word to contemporary audiences means one particular thing, though the politics it encompasses—an opposition ultimately not based in race, as Malcolm X began to point out in his last speeches after his return from Mecca, but in class—still must have seemed nearly anachronistic in the "new world order," of 1996 when this book was first published, pre-9/11, post-Gulf War, post-Oslo Accords, and, tragically, post-Rabin.

Of course she is riffing from June Jordan's poem "Moving Towards Home," in which Jordan says, "I was born a Black woman/and now/I am become a Palestinian." To say "I am become" means you are always in the ever-present moment of occurring, of being both things at once. Jordan's poem utilizes very short lines and very long lines against one another to create a poetry of rhythm in voice—very similar to the Arabic literary tradition, as exemplified by Palestinian poet Mahmoud Darwish, whose written work uses "circular prosody," a prosody that works not line by line but by sense entire throughout the poem as a whole—a poetry not unlike Hammad's, grounded in orality, in the immediacy both emotional and verbal of spoken communication. You can't fake it—its art is not from artifice but from the actual given world.

Hammad invokes June Jordan in her title, but it is more than just political solidarity that these two writers have in common. Like Jordan, Hammad can be the fiercest warrior and the tenderest whisperer, between poems, but also within a single poem, sometimes within a single line. Like Darwish on his hands and knees, crawling down the hallway of his apartment as it is bombarded, his single desire not to escape but to make it to the kitchen so he can make a pot of coffee, Hammad's real desire is to assert her humanity and humility in a world on fire.

Suheir says she makes her "own way home," and she always has. It was Suheir—within hours of the September 11th attacks, while everyone else (include me in that) was tumbling in their minds, trying to figure out what to say, and how to say it—who wrote "First Writing Since," a piece of work that traveled around the world by the speed of email, carrying our humanity, our fear, our pain, even our anger, in its lines. Suheir refused any simple sentiment in that complex, empowering, illuminating work.

It's lucky for us to have this new edition of *Born Palestinian, Born Black,* Suheir's first book, published more than ten years ago. In the decade since, Hammad has achieved an international reputation as a poet. These poems are the groundswell from which her future work and political commitment springs. Like June Jordan, like Mahmoud Darwish, it is the passion and penchant for lyricism that is the true engine of these poems, not their politics. Even at their rawest and most difficult to hear, the poems true interest lies not in the expression of anger but rather in the pure humanity of both victim and victimizer:

> did I turn your stomach?
> least I didn't turn your insides to confetti
> with a u.s. made machete up your pussy
> rape you with my machine gun down your throat
> gun point your father to molest
> you in front of my army   prostitute your essence
> til you confess you were born *phalestinian*
> confess you would die the way
> you were born   free

It is wrong to say the poems are "about" anger though anger

is part of the fabric from which they are woven. And honestly, you've got to sing these poems out loud to hear their music, but also their sense of verbal movement, even their humor.

As Brooklyn and Ramallah are connected for Hammad, as the sensations of tenderness and ferocity seem to go so hand in hand, the poems themselves buck and tumble. In "we spent fourth of july in bed," for example, the poet cannot help but meditate on the political events of the external world, saying at one point, "our sighs indeed heavy with/history   destiny   cum and responsibility/even now   in this heat/on this futon/we are not alone."

Ultimately, for this poet, as for many of her role models—to Jordan and Darwish I would add Sonia Sanchez, Mari Evans, Allen Ginsberg—one cannot really separate personal from political, or the interior and exterior worlds. The "home" she seeks is so far away, in Palestine and in the self itself at one and the same time:

> return to what we've forgotten
> what hunger has faked
> return to the whiteness of black
> to the drum   the hum   the sum of my parts
> to god   the boiling in my belly
> touch it taste   name it and
> come back to here

–Kazim Ali
Oberlin, December 2008